MEDICINAL

DONKEYS

Herbal Support for Donkeys

Eliance smith

The Power of Plants

COPY RIGHT

This book provides tools and strategies that have helped many people. However, it's important to find what works best for you, and seeking professional help can be a valuable step.

The Power of Plants

The Power of Plants

"Healing Hooves: A Donkey's Journey to health

Daisy was a kind donkey who resided in the gently sloping hills of a charming rural area. Daisy had always been a tough animal, ambling across the meadows with a deceptive elegance despite her powerful build. However, Daisy started to feel her age start to catch up with her as the seasons changed. Her once-brisk step decreased as pains started to develop in her worn-out bones. Daisy's kind farmer, Thomas, became worried when he saw her difficulties. Thomas set out to find a solution since he was determined to support his loyal friend. Veterinarians and other farmers were consulted for guidance, but none of them had a solution that would really make Daisy feel better.

Thomas once came discovered a secret garden full of colourful herbs while meandering through the verdant meadows that encircled his property. A feeling of peace enveloped him as he strolled about the garden, as if the plants themselves were whispering healing secrets. Perplexed, Thomas collected an assortment of plants and came back to Daisy's side. He made a

The Power of Plants

mixture using the healing plants he had found, using delicate hands. Doubting but optimistic, he gave Daisy the herbal cure while closely observing her for any indications of recovery. Weeks passed into days, and Thomas watched as a miracle change started to take place. Daisy's eyes brightened again, and the anguish faded, making her steps lighter. With her soul rejuvenated by the plants' therapeutic properties, she pranced across the fields once again. As news of Daisy's incredible recovery spread across the rural areas, more farmers started approaching Thomas for advice. As a team, they embraced the age-old expertise of herbal therapy, turning their farms into healing havens for their cherished animals. Daisy's voyage therefore became a monument to the remarkable relationship between people and animals as well as the amazing healing power found in nature's embrace, all set against the serene serenity of the countryside. As the years went by, Daisy's story began to inspire hope in animals everywhere. Farmers from far-off regions came to Thomas for advice, eager to master the art of herbal therapy for their own cherished pets. They came together as a community, bound by their regard for the earth's healing qualities and their mutual affection for their animals.

Daisy seemed to be bursting with energy as she wandered the fields, encouraging everyone in her path. As a live example of the transforming power of kindness and care, she came to represent resiliency and rejuvenation.

However, a shadow was hiding in the distance among the happy celebrations of Daisy's recovery. Abruptly, a terrible disease ravaged the rural areas it passed through. The ruthless hold of illness caused animals to get unwell and lose their formerly bright spirits. Thomas went to the same plants that had kept Daisy alive when he was in the depths of despair. He lovingly and hopeful applied herbal treatments to the ailing animals while tending to them with unflinching commitment. Driven by the conviction that no creature should suffer in solitude, he toiled diligently day and night. The tide started to shift gradually but steadily. The creatures began to emerge from the shadows of disease one by one, their fortitude restored by the curative power of plants. The community was united by a closer link than before as the final signs of illness vanished and a spirit of thankfulness pervaded the atmosphere.

Daisy's journey revealed how the healing power of medicinal herbs not only restored her body but also touched the hearts of everyone who saw her change. The communal spirit of compassion and resiliency had been rekindled, lighting the way forward with a bright glow of hope and healing, rather than simply the physical diseases being treated in the end.

The Power of Plants

INTRODUCTION

Since ancient times, people have revered donkeys as friends because of their kind disposition and work ethic. Like humans, they may sometimes get ill or need an all-natural boost to their health. This book explores the exciting world of therapeutic herbs for donkeys, highlighting their possible advantages and ways to enhance your donkey's overall care. But before we go into this herbal pharmacy, it's important to keep in mind that the first course of action is always to visit your veterinarian. They can guarantee that any herbs you introduce are suitable and safe for the particular requirements of your donkey.

In light of this, this book will highlight a few popular and usually safe therapeutic plants that may help your donkey on its path to better health. We'll discuss their applications, possible advantages, and even provide some advice on how to take them correctly. So grab a seat, and let's explore how the natural environment might improve your donkey's health! There is a synergy between people and animals in the picturesque settings where fields spread out beneath open sky and soft breezes dance over the grass. This

The Power of Plants

symbiotic connection is fashioned by care, compassion, and an unbreakable tie. Among the animals that inhabit these peaceful areas, the modest donkey is a representation of fortitude, tenacity, and silent camaraderie. Donkeys have been prized throughout history for their gentle nature, steadfast devotion, and their industrious labour in the fields. However, donkeys have a variety of health issues as they navigate the meandering roads of life, just like any other living thing. The healing power of natural treatments is most apparent during these times of vulnerability. Medicinal herbs have been an essential part of conventional treatment methods for ages, providing a natural, all-encompassing approach to health that recognizes the connection between the mind, body, and spirit. With the help of this book, we will go into the realm of therapeutic herbs for donkeys; this voyage will be steered by the knowledge of age-old customs and inspired by a profound respect for the earth's healing potential. We will investigate the wide range of plants that may be used to calm, bolster, and revitalize our cherished friends from the lush fields to the secret flowerbeds.

Together, we will explore the advantages and disadvantages of applying medicinal herbs to donkeys and discover safe and efficient ways to use their restorative capabilities. We will explore the diverse range of herbal treatments, learning about the special properties of each plant and how it may be used to treat donkeys. Beyond the pragmatic concerns, however, is a deeper reality, one that is based on the close relationship that exists between people, animals, and the environment that provides for all of us. It's a reality that speaks to the ageless knowledge encapsulated in the stems, leaves, and roots of the plants that adorn our landscapes; a wisdom that serves as a constant reminder of our common journey and our shared duty to preserve the fragile balance of life.

I pray that on our journey together, compassion, curiosity, and a firm commitment to the welfare of all living things—big and small—will lead us to walk softly on this planet. And may the therapeutic properties of herbs shine brightly, guiding us towards a time when plenty, peace, and well-being are the norm.

The Power of Plants

UNDERSTANDING DONKEY HEALTH

AND WELL-BEIGN

Although donkeys and horses have some traits in common, there are some small but noticeable distinctions in how donkey activity is understood. Therefore, before beginning any handling or training, it is crucial to grasp the various behaviours in general.

Donkeys connect with horses, mules, or other small stock when they are not with other donkeys, since they naturally appreciate the company of their type. Owing to their innate territoriality, acclimating cattle requires supervision and appropriate fencing. Never will a donkey from The Donkey Sanctuary be placed in an area without any other donkeys. Donkeys are known to form very deep relationships with their partners, and breaking up bonded couples may lead to enough stress for the dangerous and often deadly illness known as hyperlipaemia. Compared to horses, domesticated donkeys could be more territorial in their attitude. Because of their strong sense of territoriality, donkeys are used in many nations to protect goat and sheep flocks from wolves, foxes, dogs, and coyotes. Unfortunately, because of their territorial instincts, donkeys sometimes chase after and attack small animals like dogs, cats, sheep, and goats. Not all donkeys, however, exhibit this tendency and are able to live peacefully with these friends. Never take a chance while introducing your donkeys and other animals; instead, make sure that the process is monitored and takes many weeks.

A donkey learns from the minute it is born and keeps learning throughout its life. A foal that has been properly raised through the stages of juvenile development and socialized with other donkeys is less likely to have behavioural issues as an adult.

IMPORTANCE OF CONSULTING A

VETERINARIAN

Why, apart from you, your veterinarian is your donkey's best friend:

Given their independent spirit and stoic demeanor, donkeys may not always display obvious symptoms of suffering. Because of this, seeing a veterinarian is a crucial component of your donkey's medical regimen. The following explains why, other from you, your donkey's closest buddy is a veterinarian:

Professional Diagnosis and Treatment: Veterinarians are qualified to identify diseases and provide the best courses of action based on their education and expertise. They are able to see hidden problems that you may overlook and make sure your donkey gets the treatment they need to get back on their feet.

Preventative Care: By having routine examinations, your veterinarian may see any issues early on, when treatment is often simpler and less costly. Your veterinarian may provide advice on immunizations, dental care, and parasite control—all essential components of preventive treatment.

Tailored Attention: Donkeys have different requirements and are shaped and sized differently. Your veterinarian may create a customized treatment plan for your particular donkey based on factors including age, breed, and past medical records.

Comprehending Donkey Behaviour: Equine-trained veterinarians are familiar with the finer points of donkey behaviour. They may assist you in deciphering your donkey's indications and figuring out if anything is possibly wrong.

Peace of Mind: It is quite comforting to know that your donkey is in the capable hands of a trained specialist. You may relax knowing that you're taking every precaution to ensure the health and happiness of your pet.

Avoid Waiting Until There's an Issue

Plan on seeing your veterinarian on a frequent basis even if your donkey seems to be in good condition. The key to avoiding minor problems from becoming significant ones is early notice and care. Regard your veterinarian as an active participant in the health of your donkey.

Establishing a Bond:

It's critical for you and your donkey to have a solid rapport with your veterinarian. This enables your veterinarian to learn more about the unique personality and medical history of your donkey, resulting in better treatment. Your veterinarian is there to support you throughout this journey, so don't be afraid to ask questions or express any worries you may have.

You're giving your donkey the greatest opportunity for a long and healthy life by including veterinarian care into their regimen. In your endeavour to be the greatest donkey protector you can be, keep in mind that your veterinarian is a great resource.

BENEFITS OF MEDICINAL HERBS

The Potential Benefits of Herbal Medicine for Donkeys

Given their gentle nature and steadfast work ethic, donkeys need all the assistance we can provide to ensure their continued well-being. For these long-haired friends, medicinal herbs may be beneficial in addition to traditional veterinarian treatment. Let's see how your donkey's health might be improved by these natural remedies:

Natural Support: Adding herbs to your donkey's diet might help it feel better naturally. They could provide mild assistance for a number of systems, including the immune system, digestion, and even anxiety.

Specific Solutions: Some plants are used to treat particular ailments. For example, nettle may strengthen the immune system, while peppermint may help with unsettled stomachs.

Cost-Effective Option: Medicinal herbs may be a less expensive option for treating mild illnesses than certain prescription drugs.

Less negative Effects: In general, herbs are thought to have less negative effects than some prescription drugs. Still, it's imperative that you speak with your doctor before giving your donkey any herbs.

Crucial Points to Remember

Although using medicinal plants has its advantages, keep the following in mind:

Not a panacea: Veterinary treatment should never be replaced by herbs. Should you have any severe health issues, please contact your veterinarian right away.

Dosage Considerations: Depending on the age, weight, and overall health of the donkey, different herb dosages are recommended. The right quantity may be determined by a veterinarian.

Herb Interactions: When your donkey is receiving medicine, there are some herbs that may interfere with it. You may get advice about possible interactions from your veterinarian.

Not Every Herb Is Safe: Donkeys may be poisoned by certain plants. Introduce herbs only those that have been approved for use with horses.

Investigating Herbs Safest

Make sure to speak with your veterinarian before adding any therapeutic herbs to your donkey's regimen. Depending on the particular requirements of your donkey, they may advise you on safe and practical choices. Recall that although herbs may be a beneficial addition to your donkey's overall health regimen, they should always be administered under a trained professional's supervision.

CHAPTER ONE

COMMON HERBS FOR DONKEYS

PEPPERMINT

Uses

Peppermint for Donkeys: Calming Remedies for Intense Stomachs

Not only is peppermint a cooling plant with a stimulating scent, but it may also be a beneficial ally for donkeys who are having stomach problems. Here's a deeper look at some possible advantages of peppermint for your long-haired friend:

Calming Angry Stomachs

Peppermint's main advantage for donkeys is that it calms upset stomachs. Menthol, a substance having relaxing effects on the digestive tract, is present in the leaves. Peppermint may provide some assistance if your donkey sometimes has digestive pain, such as moderate gas or indigestion.

Methods for Dosing Peppermint

Your donkey may be fed peppermint in a few different ways:

Fresh Peppermint: Give your donkey a handful of freshly washed peppermint leaves right away. Start with a little quantity and see how they respond.

Dried Peppermint: You may add dried peppermint leaves to your donkey's grain diet or sprinkle them on top of their hay. Once again, start small and expand progressively as tolerated.

Peppermint Tea: To make a mild tea, steep a few peppermint leaves in hot water. Once cooled, present it in a bucket to your donkey.

Crucial Points to Remember

Although donkeys may safely consume peppermint in moderation, it's important to keep in mind:

Speak with your veterinarian: See your veterinarian before introducing any new food, including peppermint. They may provide guidance on the right dosage and guarantee that it won't conflict with any drugs your donkey may be on.

Begin Gradually: Always introduce peppermint gradually, and keep an eye out for any negative responses, like as colic or diarrhoea, in your donkey.

Not a panacea: Peppermint may help with sporadic stomach problems. To rule out any underlying health issues, speak with your veterinarian right away if your donkey continues to have digestive issues.

The Last Opinion on Peppermint

Given its sedative qualities, peppermint may be a natural remedy for donkeys' sporadic gastrointestinal distress. But keep in mind that you should incorporate veterinarian advice gradually and give it priority. If you use peppermint sparingly, you may be able to provide your donkey some comfort from upset stomach.

Nettle

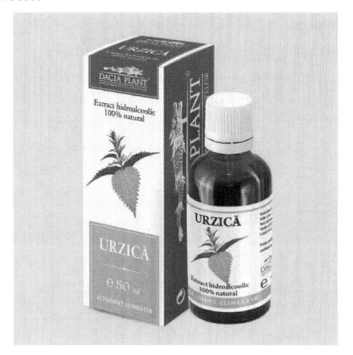

For our long-haired friends, nettles—those prickly plants we usually try to stay away from in the garden—may have surprisingly positive effects. Let's see how nettles may benefit your donkey's health:

Uses

Rich in Nutrients: Iron, calcium, magnesium, and the vitamins A, C, and K are among the many vitamins and minerals found in nettles that are important for donkey health. This increase in nutrients may promote general health.

Support for the Immune System: Research indicates that nettle may aid in bolstering the immune system. That could be a natural strategy to bolster your donkey's defenses, but more study is required.

Methods for Using Nettle

A few donkey-friendly methods for introducing nettle are as follows:

Dried Nettle: You may add dried nettle leaves to your donkey's grain diet or scatter them over their hay.

Nettle Tea: Nettle tea is made by steeping dried nettle leaves in hot water. Once cooled, present it in a bucket to your donkey. The earthy flavour could appeal to them.

Nettle Pellets: Commercially produced nettle pellets designed especially for horses and donkeys are available from certain firms. These might be a practical approach to start your donkey on nettle.

Crucial Points to Remember

Although adding nettles might be advantageous, keep in mind:

See Your Veterinarian: Speak with your veterinarian before to introducing any new food, including nettle. They may provide guidance on the right dosage and guarantee that it won't conflict with any drugs your donkey may be on.

Begin Gradually: Introduce nettle to your donkey gradually, as you would any new meal, and keep an eye out for any negative responses, such as upset stomach.

Take Care When Using New Nettles: The stinging hairs on fresh nettle leaves might hurt your donkey's lips. Choose nettle that has been dried or that has been prepared especially for animals.

Chamomile

A Soothing Friend for Donkeys: Chamomile

Renowned for its calming qualities, chamomile is a flower that resembles daisies and may help donkeys who are sometimes nervous or uncomfortable. Let's explore the possible advantages that chamomile may provide for our furry friends.

Calming Features:

Reputable for its relaxing properties is chamomile. Ingredients like apigenin may help induce relaxation by interacting with brain receptors. Chamomile may help if your donkey becomes anxious sometimes in stressful circumstances, such as while riding in a trailer or seeing the vet.

Uses

You may include chamomile into your donkey's regimen in the following ways:

Making a weak chamomile tea involves steeping dried chamomile petals in boiling water. When it cools fully, serve it in a bucket to your donkey.

One possible remedy for your donkey's drinking water problem is to administer diluted chamomile tincture. The right dilution ratio for the size of your donkey should be discussed with your veterinarian.

Companies that provide fly sprays for horses and donkeys also provide products containing chamomile. In particular, they might be a soothing choice during grooming sessions.

Important Things to Think About

Despite the fact that donkeys may safely consume chamomile in moderation, keep in mind:

See Your Veterinary Professional: Consult your veterinarian before to administering any new medication, including chamomile. For your particular donkey's requirements, they may provide advice on the right type and dose.

Commence Gradually: Proceed cautiously while adding chamomile to your recipe, keeping an eye out for any negative responses as you would with any new ingredient.

Not a Magic Bullet: For occasional anxiety, chamomile may be helpful. Contact your veterinarian to rule out any underlying health issues if your donkey consistently displays symptoms of worry.

The Chamomile Final Word

With its relaxing qualities, chamomile may be a natural way to help donkeys who become anxious sometimes. Vet advice, however, should be introduced gradually and given priority. Your pet may feel better at ease in an atmosphere you create that contains chamomile in moderation.

Milk Thistle: Potential Liver Support for Donkeys

Milk thistle, a prickly plant with purple flowers, has been traditionally used for liver health. While research on its effectiveness in donkeys is limited, let's explore its potential benefits and why consulting your veterinarian is crucial.

Uses

Liver Support: Milk thistle contains silymarin, a group of antioxidants thought to promote liver health and regeneration. This might be beneficial for donkeys recovering from liver damage or exposed to toxins.

Important Considerations

Limited Research: Studies specifically on milk thistle's effectiveness in donkeys are scarce. More research is needed to confirm its benefits for equines.

Consult Your Veterinarian: Before introducing any new supplement, including milk thistle, consult your veterinarian. They can assess your donkey's individual needs and determine if milk thistle is appropriate.

Dosage and Form: The appropriate dosage and form of milk thistle (powder, capsule, tincture) will vary depending on your donkey's weight and health condition. Your veterinarian can provide specific recommendations.

Not a Replacement for Veterinary Care: Milk thistle should not be seen as a substitute for proper veterinary diagnosis and treatment, If your donkey has liver problems, consult your veterinarian immediately.

Exploring Liver Support Options

If you're interested in supporting your donkey's liver health, your veterinarian can discuss various options, including:

Dietary Changes: Adjusting your donkey's diet to ensure they receive adequate nutrients and limit potential toxins might be the most effective approach.

Veterinary-approved Supplements: Several veterinarian-approved liver support supplements formulated specifically for horses and donkeys are available. These typically come with clear dosage instructions.

The Final Word on Milk Thistle

Milk thistle has potential benefits for liver health, but more research is needed to confirm its efficacy in donkeys. Always prioritize veterinary advice before introducing it to your donkey's routine. By working with your veterinarian, you can explore the most appropriate options to support your donkey's well-being.

Aloe Vera

Aloe Vera: A Potential Pain Reliever for Skin Wounds in Donkeys

Succulent aloe vera, prized for its calming qualities, has been used for ages to treat skin issues. Let's examine the possible advantages and the reasons why speaking with your veterinarian is so important while research on its usage in donkeys is still underway.

Uses

Aloe vera gel includes substances that may aid in the healing of wounds and lessen inflammation. Donkeys with little wounds, scratches, or abrasions could benefit from this.

Aloe vera's cooling qualities may provide some solace from the agony brought on by little skin irritations such as sunburn or bug bites.

Vital Points to Remember

Limited Research: Research on the particular benefits of aloe vera for donkey wounds is still being conducted. To validate its advantages for horses, further investigation is required.

Speak with Your Vet: See your veterinarian before using aloe vera on any wounds on your donkey. In addition to giving appropriate cleaning and treatment recommendations, they may evaluate the extent of the lesion and decide if aloe vera is appropriate.

Aloe vera is not a substitute for veterinarian treatment in cases of deep wounds or infections. See your veterinarian right away if there are any deep cuts, punctures, or wounds that exhibit symptoms of infection (pus, redness, swelling).

Digestion in Donkeys: Donkeys shouldn't eat aloe vera since it is harmful. Make sure the aloe vera gel that was put to their skin cannot be licked off or consumed.

Options for Treating Wounds

A number of products with veterinary approval have been developed especially for the treatment of wounds in horses and donkeys. Depending on the kind and extent of the wound, this may be a safer and more beneficial alternative.

The Last Word on Aloe Vera

Aloe vera may be useful for mending wounds in donkeys and relieving mild skin irritations. Prioritize veterinarian guidance before applying it to your donkey, however. You can make sure that your donkey's skin issues are treated in the safest and most efficient way possible by collaborating with your veterinarian.

Echinacea

The flowering herb Echinacea, which is well-known for enhancing the immune system, may assist donkeys in the following ways:

Uses

Immune Support: Echinacea may strengthen the immune system in donkeys, just as it does in people. This may be especially helpful when things are stressful, as when the weather or environment changes or when additional animals are added to the herd. Donkeys that have higher immune systems are better able to fend off infections and diseases.

Wound Healing: Because of its anti-inflammatory and antibacterial qualities, Echinacea has long been used to aid in the healing of wounds. Applying Echinacea physically or giving it orally to donkeys may aid in their wound, cut, and abrasion healing processes.

Health of the Respiratory System: Just like other animals, donkeys may have respiratory diseases. By bolstering the body's natural defense systems, Echinacea's immune-stimulating qualities may help prevent or lessen the severity of respiratory diseases in donkeys.

Stress Reduction: A donkey's diet or health regimen may benefit from using Echinacea to lessen the impacts of stress. The adaptogenic qualities of Echinacea may aid donkeys in managing stress better whether it arises from changes in schedule, transportation, or other environmental variables.

Gastrointestinal Health: According to some studies, Echinacea may improve digestive performance and maintain a balanced population of gut flora in the gastrointestinal tract. This might be especially crucial for donkeys that are prone to digestive problems like diarrhoea or colic.

Overall Well-Being: Adding Echinacea to a donkey's daily routine of care may enhance their resilience and overall well-being. Echinacea can strengthen the immune system and general health of donkeys, enabling them to enjoy long and healthy lives.

Notably, Echinacea may have certain advantages, but before adding any new supplement or herbal therapy to a donkey's diet or medical regimen, it's crucial to speak with a veterinarian. For safety and efficacy, appropriate dose and administration techniques must also be used.

The Power of Plants

1.1 Garlic

Garlic: A Fragrant Companion with Possible Advantages for Donkeys

The pungent plant garlic, which enhances the flavour of our food, may also have some benefits for our donkey friends. Remembering the value of veterinarian advice, let's examine the possible advantages and disadvantages of garlic for donkeys.

Uses

Insect Repellent: Research indicates that horses and donkeys who eat garlic may be able to keep off certain flies and mosquitoes. For donkeys with delicate skin, this could be particularly helpful during fly season.

Internal Parasite Support: Garlic may have some minor internal parasite-repelling effects, according to certain study. It should not, however, be used in place of the routine deworming procedures that your veterinarian advises.

Overall Support: Antioxidants and immune-boosting substances are only two of the many chemicals found in garlic that may have positive effects on health. Nonetheless, further investigation is required to validate these advantages particularly in donkeys.

Crucial Points to Remember

Dosage Matters: Depending on the donkey's age, weight, and overall health, there are different guidelines for how much garlic is recommended. Overindulging them in garlic might be dangerous.

Speak with your veterinarian: See your veterinarian before adding garlic to your donkey's diet. They are able to calculate the right dose and make sure it won't conflict with any drugs your donkey may be on.

Possible Adverse Reactions: Donkeys with high garlic intakes may get digestive disturbances. Start with a tiny dose and keep an eye out for any negative side effects, such as colic or diarrhoea.

Not a Miracle Treatment It is not appropriate to think of garlic as a panacea for all medical issues, For an accurate diagnosis and course of action in the event that your donkey has fly difficulties, parasite problems, or any other health issues, speak with your veterinarian.

How to Introduce Garlic Safely:

Here are some choices to consider if your donkey's veterinarian approves of adding garlic to its diet:

Small cloves of fresh garlic, chopped finely, should be added to your donkey's grain diet (Limited Amounts).

Garlic Powder: Sprinkle your donkey's meal with a little quantity at first, and then increase as acceptable.

Supplements prepared commercially: There are businesses that sell veterinarian-approved supplements made especially for horses and donkeys. Usually, they have precise dose recommendations.

The Last Word Regarding Garlic

Donkeys may benefit from the insect repellent and moderate internal parasite assistance that garlic may provide. Prioritize speaking with your veterinarian before adding anything new to your donkey's diet, however. They can guarantee it won't hurt and provide advice on safe doses. You may investigate the best choices to maintain your donkey's comfort and well-being by consulting with your veterinarian.

Donkey Marshmallow Root: A Calm Choice for Allergic Stomachs (But First, See Your Vet!)

For donkeys suffering from stomach pain, marshmallow root, a flowering plant with a long history of medical usage, may provide some help. But like with other herbal medicines, it's important to speak with your veterinarian before administering it. Here's a deeper look at the possible advantages and the reasons getting veterinary advice is crucial.

Uses

Calming inflamed Tissues: Mucilage, a gel-like material found in marshmallow root, has the ability to cover and calm inflamed digestive system tissues. Donkeys with periodic heartburn or minor stomach discomfort may benefit from this.

Crucial Points to Remember
Limited Research: There are few studies particularly examining the benefits of marshmallow root for donkeys. To prove its advantages for horse digestion, further study is required.

Speak with your veterinarian: See your veterinarian before to administering any new medication, including marshmallow root. They may evaluate the specific requirements of your donkey and decide if marshmallow root is a good fit.

Form and Dosage: The right amount of marshmallow root (powder, tincture, etc.) and its shape will depend on the size and overall health of your donkey. You can get particular advice from your veterinarian.

Not a panacea: It is not appropriate to use marshmallow root in place of a qualified veterinarian's diagnosis and care. To rule out any underlying health issues, speak with your veterinarian right away if your donkey continues to have digestive issues.

Options Other Than Digestive Support

The digestive health of your donkey may be supported by a number of veterinarian-approved options:

Dietary Changes: The best course of action may be to modify your donkey's food to guarantee that they get enough fiber and to reduce any possible irritants.

Probiotics: Supplementing with veterinarian-approved probiotics may assist optimize digestion by reestablishing a healthy balance of gut microorganisms.

Veterinary Medication: To treat the underlying cause of more serious digestive problems, your veterinarian may recommend certain drugs.

The Marshmallow Root Final Word

There may be advantages to marshmallow root for donkeys with minor gastric distress, But before you introduce it, give veterinarian advice priority. You may investigate the best solutions to take care of your donkey's digestive issues and maintain their general wellbeing by consulting with your veterinarian.

The Power of Plants

Peppermint

Peppermint: A Calm Remedy for Angry Donkey Stomachs

The cooling plant renowned for its energizing scent, peppermint, may also be a valuable ally for donkeys who sometimes have digestive problems. The following is a summary of the possible advantages of peppermint for your long-haired friend:

Uses

Calming Upset Stomachs: Peppermint's main advantage for donkeys is its capacity to calm upset stomachs, Menthol, a substance having relaxing effects on the digestive tract, is present in the leaves.

Peppermint may help with occasional gas, moderate indigestion, and other digestive pain in your donkey.

Methods for Dosing Peppermint:

Several donkey-friendly methods exist for including peppermint into their diet:

Fresh Peppermint: Give your donkey a handful of freshly washed peppermint leaves right away. Start with a little quantity and see how they respond.

Dried Peppermint: You may add dried peppermint leaves to your donkey's grain diet or sprinkle them on top of their hay. Start with a little amount and raise it progressively as tolerated.

Peppermint Tea: To make a mild tea, steep a few peppermint leaves in hot water. Once cooled, present it in a bucket to your donkey.

Crucial Points to Remember:

Although donkeys may safely consume peppermint in moderation, keep in mind:

Speak with your veterinarian: See your veterinarian before introducing any new food, including peppermint. They may provide guidance on the right dosage and guarantee that it won't conflict with any drugs your donkey may be on.

Begin Gradually: Always introduce peppermint gradually, and keep an eye out for any negative responses, like as colic or diarrhoea, in your donkey.

Not a panacea: Peppermint may help with sporadic stomach problems. To rule out any underlying health issues, speak with your veterinarian right away if your donkey continues to have digestive issues.

The Last Opinion on Peppermint:

Given its sedative qualities, peppermint may be a natural remedy for donkeys' sporadic gastrointestinal distress. But keep in mind that you should incorporate veterinarian advice gradually and give it priority. If you use peppermint sparingly, you may be able to provide your donkey some comfort from upset stomach.

Turmeric

Donkeys may benefit from the use of turmeric, the golden spice that is well-known for its vivid colour and anti-inflammatory qualities. The usefulness of turmeric for donkeys is still being studied, but let's reviews what we now know and why speaking with your veterinarian is so important.

Uses

Curcumin, a substance with anti-inflammatory qualities, is present in turmeric. For donkeys with injuries or illnesses like arthritis that cause joint pain or inflammation, this may be helpful.

Important Things to Think About:

Research Gap: There are few studies that particularly examine the benefits of turmeric for donkeys. Its advantages must be confirmed, and the right doses must be determined by further study.

The body finds it difficult to absorb curcumin, the therapeutic ingredient found in turmeric, due to its limited bioavailability. Enhancing absorption may be possible with certain formulations or by mixing turmeric and black pepper.

See Your Veterinary Professional: Get advice from your veterinarian before adding turmeric to your donkey's diet. They can evaluate if turmeric is a good choice after evaluating your donkey's specific requirements.

Dosage and Form: Depending on your donkey's size and health, there are many forms and dosages of turmeric (powder, extract, etc.). There are certain suggestions that your veterinarian may make.

Possible interactions: There's a chance that certain drugs your donkey is taking may interact with turmeric. Advice on possible interactions may be obtained from your veterinarian.

Various Options for Collaborative Assistance

You may help your donkey's joint health with a few veterinarian-approved options:

Supplements created by veterinarians: A variety of joint supplements designed especially for horses and donkeys are accessible. These usually include components that support joint health, such as chondroitin and glucosamine.

Weight Control: By keeping your donkey within a healthy weight range, you can ease the strain on their joints.

Exercise Routines: Consistently engaging in low-impact physical activity may aid in preserving joint strength and flexibility.

Lastly, some thoughts on turmeric

Its anti-inflammatory qualities make turmeric a promising remedy for donkeys with joint problems. Before introducing it, however, give your veterinarian's advice first priority. You may choose the best course of action to promote the joint health and general wellbeing of your donkey by consulting with your doctor.

CHAPTER TWO

ADDITIONAL CONSIDERATIONS

2.1 HERBS TO AVOID IN DONKEYS

The following is a list of plants that are **usually regarded as dangerous or that may be harmful to donkeys:**

Black walnut: Donkeys may be poisoned by black walnut, despite the fact that it is sometimes used to deworm horses.

Bracken Fern: The poisons in bracken fern may harm a donkey's kidneys and digestive tract. Datura Stramonium, often known as Jimson Weed, is an extremely poisonous psychoactive plant that may kill donkeys by causing convulsions, hallucinations, and other symptoms.

Milkweed: A number of milkweed species are poisonous to donkeys, resulting in unsettled stomachs and maybe even neurological issues.

Oleander: Donkeys risk death if they consume any portion of the very deadly oleander plant.

Pokeweed: The chemicals in this ubiquitous weed may make donkeys throw up, have diarrhoea, or have respiratory issues.

White snakeroot: This blooming plant may give donkey's milk sickness, a potentially lethal illness.

Important Information

There may be more plants that are harmful to donkeys; this is not a complete list. Any plant should always be identified before letting your donkey graze on it. Err on the side of caution and seek a veterinarian or a trustworthy source of information on donkey health, such a university extension office or a donkey breed society, if you're uncertain about a specific plant.

Here are some safer options to think about:

Nettle: Packed with vitamins and minerals, nettle may provide significant nutritional value to a donkey's diet (as long as it is given under a veterinarian's supervision).

Peppermint: When used sparingly, peppermint helps relieve donkeys' sporadic stomach distress.

Chamomile: In times of stress, this soothing plant may provide some respite for nervous donkeys.

Recall:

It is imperative that you speak with your veterinarian before adding any new herbs to your donkey's diet. They can provide safe choices and guarantee that the herb won't conflict with any prescriptions your donkey may be on.

The Power of Plants

2.2 RECOGNIZING SIGNS OF ADVERSE REACTIONS

Identifying Adverse Reaction Symptoms in Donkeys: Stay Vigilant and Respond Quickly

Given their stoic demeanour, donkeys may not always display obvious symptoms of suffering. For this reason, it's critical to maintain vigilance and spot any warning indications of negative responses. You may reduce any bad effects and make sure your donkey gets medical care on time by taking swift action.

The following are some things to be aware of:

Digestive Problems: Your donkey may be reacting to anything it has eaten if it is exhibiting symptoms of diarrhoea, constipation, colic (abdominal discomfort), or decreased appetite.

Skin Issues: Reactions to topical medications or items they come into touch with may manifest as skin irritation, itching, rashes, or compulsive licking of a specific region.

Behavioural Modifications: Unusual hostility, despair, lethargy, or vocalizations outside of typical behaviour might all be indicators of discomfort.

Breathing difficulties, coughing, or wheezing may be signs of a respiratory response to an irritant that has been inhaled.

Neurological Signs: Serious symptoms including tremors, seizures, weakness, or loss of coordination may need to be attended to by a veterinarian right once.

After adding a new item (food, herb, or prescription) to your donkey's routine, if you see any of these symptoms, follow these instructions:

Put an end to the source: Take the suspected offender out of your donkey's surroundings right away.

Get in touch with your veterinarian: Give your veterinarian a call as soon as possible and fully describe the circumstances. It would be preferable if they evaluated your donkey sooner.

Record Everything: Note everything that happened, including the drug introduced, when it was introduced, and any symptoms that were seen. Your veterinarian will find this information useful in determining the cause of the response.

The Key Is Prevention

Grazing Management: Make sure the meadows where your donkey grazes are devoid of any toxic plants. Seek expert assistance for plant identification if you have any doubts about any plants in their grazing area.

Present Novel Ideas Gradually: Start with a very little quantity of any new food, herb, or prescription, and keep a cautious eye out for any responses in your donkey.

Veterinarian Advice: Before adding any new items to your donkey's diet or routine, always get advice from your veterinarian. Regarding hazards and safe choices, they may provide advice.

Your donkey's health and well-being may be guaranteed and the likelihood of negative responses reduced by exercising caution and adopting preventative action. Keep in mind that treating any health issues your pet may have requires early notice and action.

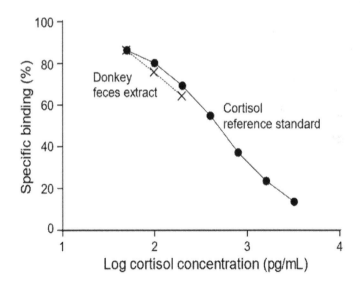

2.3 COMBINING HERBS WITH MEDICATIONS

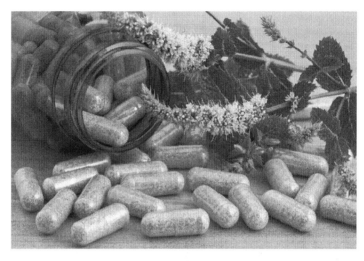

It's important to use care and seek veterinarian advice when combining herbs with pharmaceuticals for donkeys. This is the reason it's important to speak with your veterinarian before giving any herbs in addition to prescription drugs:

Possible Correspondences

Diminished Effectiveness: Certain herbs have the ability to obstruct the metabolism or absorption of drugs, reducing their efficacy.

Increased Side Effects: Occasionally, herbs might make prescription side effects worse, putting your donkey through pain or even very serious issues.

The Significance of Determining the Herb and Drug

The particular characteristics of each drug and plant determine the consequences that will result from mixing them. This is why it's crucial to see your veterinarian:

Comprehending Herbal Properties: Your veterinarian can determine if a certain herb might interfere with any medicine your donkey is already on.

Dosage Considerations: The quantity of the plant you are thinking about using might also affect possible interactions. If your veterinarian thinks it's suitable to mix the herb with the prescription, they can calculate a safe dose.

Safer Substitutes

Supplements recommended or carried by veterinarians: A lot of veterinarians carry or suggest certain supplements designed for donkeys. These are often made from herbs, but they undergo testing and processing to guarantee their safety and suitability for use with popular drugs.

Dietary Modifications: Often, the problem you're attempting to solve with herbs may be resolved with dietary modifications. Rather of taking herbs along with medicine, your veterinarian may provide advice on dietary changes that may be safer and more beneficial.

The Last Word on Taking Herbs and Drugs Together:

Although herbs may have some advantages for donkeys, when they are on medicine, it is important to prioritize veterinarian guidance. In order to minimize the possibility of drug interactions while addressing your donkey's health issues, your veterinarian might suggest safe and effective alternatives. Never forget that your donkey's welfare comes first!

CHAPTER THREE

RESOURCES

3.1 REPUTABLE SOURCES FOR EQUINE HERBS

It is essential to locate reliable suppliers of equine herbs for donkeys in order to guarantee the goods' quality and safety. Here are a few trustworthy places where you may get premium herbs made especially for donkeys:

Veterinary Advice: Speak with a vet who focuses on the health of horses. They may provide expert guidance on which herbs are best for your donkey's particular requirements and could suggest reliable manufacturers or suppliers.

Equine Herbalists: Consult with licenced equine herbalists who are skilled in creating herbal treatments for donkeys and horses. Based on your donkey's particular needs and health state, they may provide tailored advice.

Verified Herbal Providers: Seek for providers or businesses that focus on offering herbs and herbal products especially for horses. Make sure they get their herbs from reliable vendors or farmers and follow quality control guidelines.

Equine Nutritionists: Seek advice from equine nutritionists who are familiar with donkey nutritional requirements. They may provide advice on dose and administration as well as appropriate herbs to add to your donkey's diet.

Herbal Books and Publications: Read credible books, journals, and publications authored by subject-matter specialists on horse herbalism. These sites often include insightful details on the use, dosing, and safety precautions of several herbs for donkeys. Online Communities and Forums: Participate in online communities and forums devoted to donkey care and equine herbal medicines. Ask other donkey owners who have successfully employed herbs for their animals for advice and firsthand accounts of their experiences.

Local Farmers or Herbalists: Occasionally, local farmers or herbalists may sell plants suitable for horses, even donkeys. To preserve the freshness and potency of the herbs, make sure they are collected responsibly and produced organically.

Third-party Certifications: Seek for herbs that have undergone testing or certification by a third party for potency, purity, and lack of impurities. A certification that guarantees quality and safety is the USDA Organic or Good Manufacturing Practices (GMP).

It's crucial to do in-depth research, ask questions, and confirm the reputation and legitimacy of the provider or source when purchasing herbs for your donkey. Additionally, before adding any new herbs or supplements to your donkey's diet or medical routine, always seek the advice of a veterinarian or other certified equine practitioner.

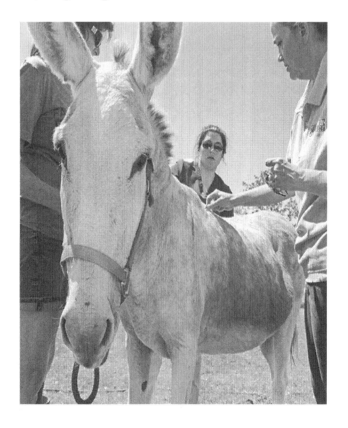

3.2 DONKEY HEALTH ORGANIZATIONS

Here are some reputable Donkey Health Organizations:

- **The Donkey Sanctuary (https://www.thedonkeysanctuary.org.uk/)** is the world's largest charity for donkeys and mules. They provide sanctuary to over 4,000 donkeys and mules, and also work to improve the lives of donkeys and mules worldwide through veterinary care, education, and advocacy.

Donkey Sanctuary

The Brooke (https://www.thebrooke.org/) is another international animal welfare charity that works specifically to improve the lives of working equines. They provide veterinary care, training, and education to working donkey and mule owners in some of the world's poorest countries.

Brooke Organization

The American Donkey and Mule Society (https://www.lovelongears.com/) is a nonprofit organization dedicated to the promotion of donkeys and mules. They offer a variety of resources on donkey care, including information on health, nutrition, and training.

The Donkey Welfare Trust (https://www.thedonkeysanctuary.org.uk/for m/contact-us-welfare-enquiries) is a UK-based charity that works to improve the welfare of donkeys worldwide. They provide veterinary care, education, and advocacy for donkeys.

Donkey Welfare Trust

The SPANA (https://spana.org/) is an animal welfare charity that works to improve the lives of animals in developing countries. They provide veterinary care, education, and advocacy for a variety of animals, including donkeys.

The Power of Plants

CONCLUSION

The Last Word on Giving Herbs to Donkeys: Put Safety First and Consult Your Vet

Donkeys are delicate creatures that need our greatest attention. Although herbs have long been used to treat a variety of ailments, the most important thing to keep in mind when using them for your long-haired friend is safety.

Observe the following

Speak with Your Veterinarian: Get advice from your veterinarian before adding any new herbs to your donkey's diet. They are able to evaluate the particular requirements of your donkey, make sure the herb is safe, and calculate the right dose.

Not a Stand-In for Veterinary Treatment: Herbs are not a panacea and shouldn't take the place of a qualified veterinarian's diagnosis and care. See your vet right away if your donkey starts having health issues.

Possible Dangers: Donkeys may be poisonous to certain plants, even in little doses. Safer substitutes Supplements and food changes recommended by veterinarians may be safer and more efficient ways to treat your donkey's health issues.

The favourable tidings?
Natural Approach: Herbs may provide a natural way to assist your donkey's health when handled properly.

There Are Safe Herbs Available: Donkeys may benefit from the use of several herbs, such as chamomile, peppermint, and nettle (under veterinarian supervision).

When appropriate, you may collaborate with your veterinarian to find safe and efficient ways to support your donkey's health using natural methods. Recall that having a happy and healthy donkey around is a pleasure, and attaining it requires proper care.

Made in United States
Troutdale, OR
11/26/2024

25272990R00040